PLIGHT OF THE PELICAN

How Science Saved a Species

BY

Jessica Stremer

ILLUSTRATED BY

Gordy Wright

books for a better earth™

holiday house • new york

For millions of years, pelicans have flown over Earth,

skimming the salty sea breeze,

then climbing

    higher

      and

        higher

          searching

          spotting

        diving

      down

    down

SPLASH!

scoop

gulp.

But in the 1950s,

something put their future at risk.

With every

SPLASH

scoop

gulp,

something was silently staying,

silently building.

4

Fewer pelican chicks were born.

And pelicans weren't the only ones.

The number of bald eagles,

raptors,

and many other birds of prey plunged

lower

and

lower.

Scientists noticed.

And they worried:

Would there come a day

when pelicans were gone

forever?

Scientists ran tests, but could not find out why bird numbers were dropping.

They kept searching until they found a clue.

When brooding parents sat warming,

waiting,

the usually strong eggshells

did not support the parents' weight.

CRACK

BREAK!

Scientists needed to find out,

why?

before it was too late.

More sampling,

testing,

and making connections.

AHA!

10

Scientists detected

    a chemical called DDT,

sprayed by farmers

to rid their crops of pesky insects,

in each of the samples.

In the water,

in the soil,

    even in animals the pelicans ate.

All throughout the food web,

DDT was there,

building

building

building

inside birds' bodies,

causing eggshells

to become

weaker

and

weaker.

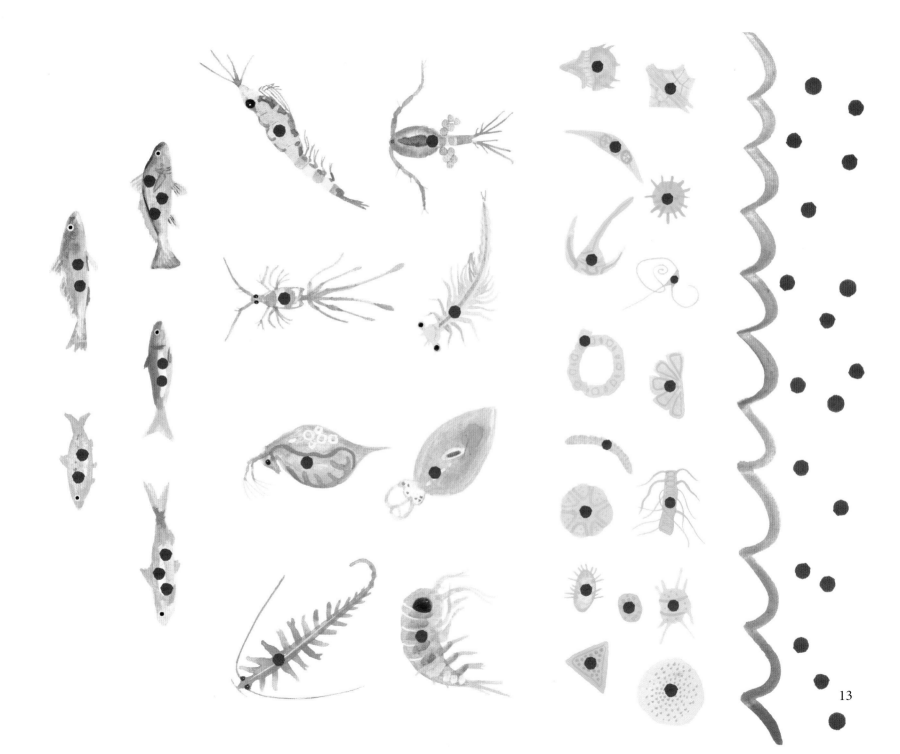

13

14

To try and help pelicans survive,

scientists removed some from the wild,

placed them in zoos,

and fed them food free of DDT.

Fragile eggs were warmed away from parents

so shells wouldn't

crack   and   break.

Scientists pleaded with farmers and the government,

STOP THE SPRAYING!

Would anyone listen?

The farmers worried about insects.
Without DDT, they would

chomp

devour

and destroy crops.

18

The people who made the chemical
said the scientists' findings were fake.

The government believed that
because this chemical had been used for years,
surely,
    it was safe.
They didn't listen to scientists.
    Until . . .

One scientist wrote a book

about springs

when songbirds would no longer sing.

About a chemical building,

eggshells thinning,

and chicks no longer hatching.

She shared ways DDT hurt

bees,

butterflies,

cows,

    and even people.

And the more she wrote . . .

the more people listened.

The number of birds continued to drop

lower

and

lower

while people

demanding change grew

louder

and

louder

until . . .

21

the government had no choice

      but to take action.

They passed a law

making it a crime to spray certain chemicals.

Pelicans,

and many more creatures

who were at risk of disappearing from Earth,

were added to a special list.

More laws,

more protection for endangered animals

and for the places these animals lived.

      Could pelicans be saved?

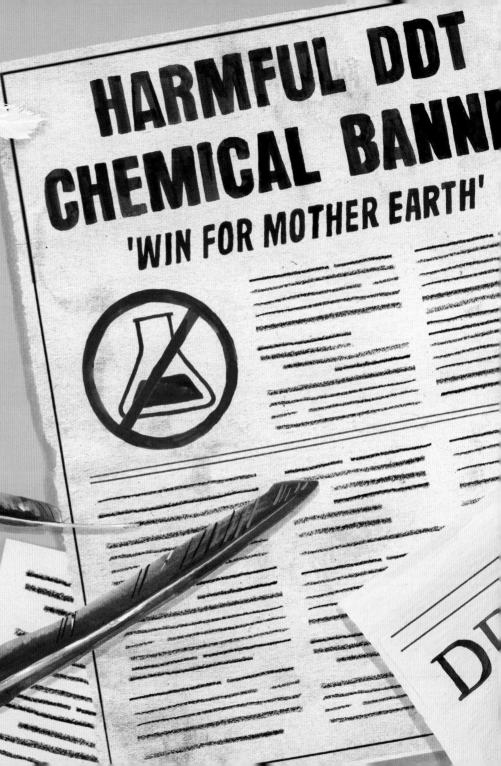

The Daily News

PESTICIDE RULED ENVIRONMENTAL HAZARD

December, 1972

Total Ban Announced

Without the harmful chemical entering the food web, no longer silently building,

generation

after

generation,

pelican eggshells became strong enough to support the weight of their parents.

People celebrated more and more chicks
            flapping   flying
hatching   lifting   SURVIVING.

Nearly thirty-seven years after people stopped spraying

    the silently harmful,

    silently building chemical,

the number of pelicans went

high enough

        up

      up

   up

that they were no longer at risk

of disappearing.

But the destruction of forests,

building of man-made structures,

and overhunting

　　meant others were not as fortunate.

27

Today,

as pelicans skim the salty sea breeze,

climbing

diving

SPLASHING

scooping,

the list of plants and animals at risk

of disappearing from Earth

     grows

         and

             grows.

28

Pollinators dwindle as food sources disappear.

Songbirds struggle to find a suitable spot to hatch their young.

Marine life gobble garbage.

Yet there is hope.

Thanks to the pelicans, we know a bit about what works in the fight for our future. The fight against warming weather and disappearing homes.

By figuring out *why* a species struggles,

scientists can take action to help them.

From making safer products,

to creating wildlife corridors,

protecting critical habitats,

and reintroducing animals to their native ranges,

scientists continue to study,

invent,

find solutions,

and learn from our mistakes

while people just like you

use their voice

louder

and

louder

to stand up,

speak out,

and inspire change.

31

The chemical DDT was created in 1874. Farmers used it to kill insects that spread disease to humans and damage crops. DDT was also sometimes dumped into rivers, mixed in with wastewater from manufacturing facilities.

The more chemical people sprayed, the more it remained in the ground, harming plants and animals. Small animals at the center of the food web died from DDT and were eaten by other animals further out in the food web. While DDT didn't outright kill the larger predators, it built up in their tissues and harmed their bodies.

A scientist named Rachel Carson wrote a book explaining how DDT was not only hurting birds but other animals in the ecosystem as well. Many people didn't believe Rachel. They liked that DDT protected their crops and farm animals, and that the chemical killed insects that spread disease.

The chemical makers wanted people to keep using DDT since it made them money. Even when some people suspected DDT was harmful to humans, the chemical makers pressed on.

Rachel wrote newspaper articles in hopes that more people would learn about the harmful effects of DDT. Her words were her voice, and the more the government ignored scientists' findings, the louder Rachel got.

Because of Rachel, people learned how all things in nature are connected. People realized that things they did, like spraying poisonous chemicals, affected plants and animals in ways they couldn't see.

Communities came together and asked the government to do something about the use of DDT. At first, the government sided with the chemical manufacturers. But scientists, Rachel, and many other people refused to back down. Eventually, the government had no choice but to take action.

In 1966, the government passed the Endangered Species Preservation Act. It was a step in the right direction but did little to actually stop people from harming animals or destroying their habitats. The act was expanded a year later to include a broad list of endangered animals. However, it did not include any plants, and it still lacked consequences for people violating the act.

Finally, in 1970, the government created the Environmental Protection Agency (EPA). The EPA allowed the government to hold the people who purposely harmed endangered animals or destroyed places where these animals lived accountable for their actions. The EPA also funded programs to solve pollution problems through research and education.

Then in 1973, the government passed a powerful law called the Endangered Species Act (ESA), which added flowers, grasses, and trees to the growing list of threatened or endangered species. Many of these organisms suffered from overhunting, habitat loss, and predation by invasive species.

With the creation of the ESA, scientists could now work with the government to find solutions and stop human actions that could cause populations of at-risk plants and animals to decrease even more. The ESA also created guidelines for when a species should be added or removed from the Endangered Species List.

Today, the Endangered Species List is used by members of the EPA and conservation groups around the world to identify biological hotspots, guide research, create conservation plans, influence policies to better protect threatened wildlife, and provide education about and awareness of species conservation efforts.

For a current list of threatened or endangered plants and animals, visit:

www.fws.gov/program/endangered-species
www.iucnredlist.org
www.worldwildlife.org/species/directory

BE THE CHANGE

- Plant a pollinator garden

- Build a bird or bat house (or both!)

- Help your parents check their vehicle for leaks

- Throw trash in the garbage can, and pick up litter you find lying on the ground

- Participate in a community cleanup

- Recycle and reuse items

- Write to members of the government and ask them to increase protection for animals, and specifically to find alternatives to toxic chemicals being used today

HOW DDT HURTS BIRDS

When the number of brown pelicans and other birds of prey began decreasing, scientists thought it had something to do with their ability to reproduce. Scientists examined and ran tests on adult birds but couldn't find anything physically wrong with their ability to fertilize and lay eggs.

Scientists ran more tests, which revealed high amounts of DDT in birds' blood. But brown pelicans, bald eagles, and raptors weren't directly sprayed with the chemical itself. So how did it get into their bodies?

To confirm their suspicions, scientists performed toxicity testing on soil and water samples, as well as on insects, fish, and various animals. They found DDT in each of the samples. And the farther the organism was from the center of the food web, the more DDT they found.

The final piece to the puzzle was put into place when scientists discovered that DDT reduced the transfer of calcium in birds' blood to their developing eggs. Less calcium caused shells to become weak and unable to withstand the weight of adult birds.

Unfortunately, many toxic chemicals stay in the environment for years and years, and there's no way to remove them from an organism once it has entered their body (either by being absorbed or eaten). The only way to stop chemicals from causing harm is to no longer use them.

MORE ABOUT BROWN PELICANS

- A group of pelicans is called a squadron.

- When pelicans fly low over the water, they save energy by not flapping their wings.

- When pelicans get hungry, they climb high above the water to search for food. Pelicans eat mostly fish, but will eat turtles, crustaceans, and other birds if necessary.

- Pelicans dive from as high as sixty-five feet in the air. They have special sacs beneath their skin that inflate just before they hit the water. These sacs protect the pelican from getting hurt, like airbags in cars protect people.

- A pelican's pouch holds nearly three gallons of water. Pelicans drain the water just before swallowing their catch.

- Males swing their head from side to side to attract a female, then gather materials such as grass, leaves, and twigs for females to build a nest.

- On average, the female lays three eggs each season. Eggs hatch twenty-nine to thirty-five days after being laid.

- Baby pelicans rely on their parents for food and protection. The chick's first meal is food their parents have swallowed and then thrown up.

- Pelicans learn to fly when they are three months old. When they are fully grown, their wings can spread up to 6.5 feet wide.

- Pelicans use their long bill to spread a special oil over their wings and head. This oil keeps their feathers clean and dry.

GLOSSARY

Ban – A rule against using something.

Bioaccumulation – When a harmful substance builds up in the tissues of an organism.

Biological Hot Spot – An area that contains multiple at-risk plants or animals.

Ecosystem – The living (plants and animals) and nonliving (water, rocks, etc.) things that exist and interact with one another in a given area.

Endangered – Plants or animals that are on the verge of disappearing forever.

Extinct – A plant or animal that no longer exists.

Food Web – Links animals together to show how they get their food.

Threatened – A plant or animal that is close to going extinct.

BIBLIOGRAPHY

Carson, Rachel. *Silent Spring*. London: Penguin Books, in association with Hamish Hamilton, 2015.

"DDT (Technical Fact Sheet)." National Pesticide Information Center. Last modified 2000. https://npic.orst .edu/factsheets/archive/ddttech.pdf.

Ehrlich, Paul R., David S. Dobkin, and Darryl Wheye. "DDT and Birds." DDT and Birds. Stanford, 1988. https://web.stanford.edu/group/stanfordbirds/text /essays/DDT_and_Birds.html.

"Endangered Species: U.S. Fish & Wildlife Service." FWS.gov. https://www.fws.gov/program /endangered-species/about-us.

"Endangered Species Act | U.S. Fish & Wildlife Service." U.S. Fish and Wildlife Service. https://www.fws.gov/law /endangered-species-act.

"Endangered Species Act Milestones: Pre 1973." FWS.gov. https://fws.gov/node/266462.

Harada, T., Takeda, M., Kojima, S., Tomiyama, N. "Toxicity and Carcinogenicity of Dichlorodiphenyltrichloroethane (DDT)." *Toxicol Res*. 32, (January 2016): 21–33. https:// doi.org/10.5487/TR.2016.32.1.021

Lipske, Michael. "How Rachel Carson Helped Save the Brown Pelican." National Wildlife Federation, December 1, 1999. https://www.nwf.org/Magazines /National-Wildlife/2000/How-Rachel-Carson -Helped-Save-The-Brown-Pelican#:~:text=California's %20pelicans%20were%20not%20killed,instead%20 squashed%20them%20into%20omelettes.

Rothman, Lily. "Environmental Protection Agency: Why the EPA Was Created." Time. March 22, 2017. https://time.com/4696104/environmental-protection -agency-1970-history/.

"Summary of the Endangered Species Act." US EPA. Last modified September 28, 2021. https://www.epa.gov /laws-regulations/summary-endangered-species-act.

"The Case of DDT: Revisiting the Impairment." US EPA. Last modified July 12, 2022. https://www.epa.gov /caddis-vol1/case-ddt-revisiting-impairment.

"The Origins of the EPA." EPA. Environmental Protection Agency. July 9, 2021. https://www.epa.gov/history /origins-epa.

"U.S. Fish and Wildlife Service Proposes Delisting 23 Species from Endangered Species Act Due to Extinction." U.S. Department of the Interior. Last modified September 29, 2021. https://www.doi.gov/pressreleases/us-fish-and -wildlife-service-proposes-delisting-23-species -endangered-species-act-due.

INDEX

To Dad, the answer is always yes —J. S.
To Tim Knights —G. W.

A Books for a Better Earth™ Title

The Books for a Better Earth™ collection is designed to inspire young people to become active, knowledgeable participants in caring for the planet they live on. Focusing on solutions to climate change challenges, the collection looks at how scientists, activists, and young leaders are working to safeguard Earth's future.

Library of Congress Cataloging-in-Publication Data

Names: Stremer, Jessica, author. | Wright, Gordy, illustrator.
Title: Plight of the pelican : how science saved a species / by Jessica Stremer ; illustrated by Gordy Wright.
Description: First edition. | New York, New York : Holiday House, [2025]
Series: Books for a better Earth | Includes bibliographical references
and index. | Audience: Ages 5-8 | Audience: Grades K-1 | Summary:
"A nonfiction picture book that chronicles the science and activism that
not only saved the pelicans in the 1950s but led to the founding of the
EPA and the Endangered Species Act"–Provided by publisher.
Identifiers: LCCN 2024016003 | ISBN 9780823457038 (hardcover)
Subjects: LCSH: Endangered species–Juvenile literature. | Wildlife
conservation–Juvenile literature. | Pelicans–Juvenile literature.
Carson, Rachel, 1907-1964. Silent spring–Juvenile literature.
Classification: LCC QL83 .S67 2025 | DDC 591.68–dc23/eng/20240529
LC record available at https://lccn.loc.gov/2024016003

ISBN: 978-0-8234-5703-8 (hardcover)

EU Authorized Representative: HackettFlynn Ltd, 36 Cloch Choirneal, Balrothery, Co.
Dublin, K32 C942, Ireland. EU@walkerpublishinggroup.com